name & date

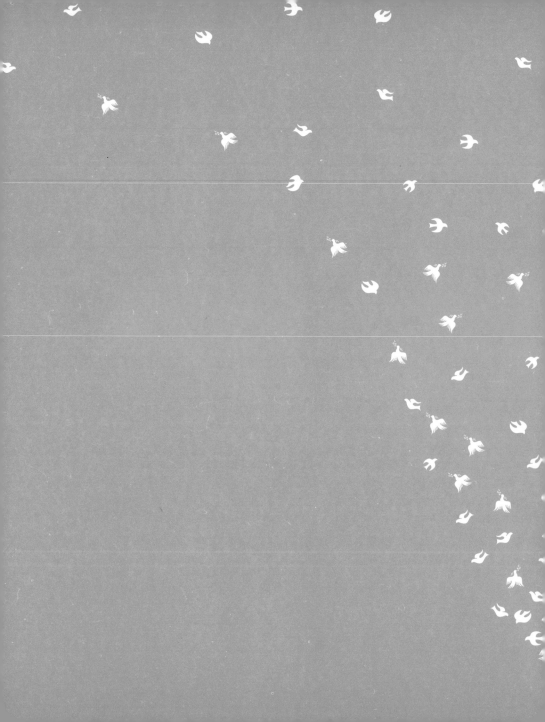

o u r   p r a y e r

"OUR PRAYER IS THAT THE DAUGHTERS OF PLANET EARTH WOULD KNOW HOW VALUED AND IMPORTANT THEY ARE; THAT THE POTENTIAL WITHIN EACH WOMAN WILL EMERGE AND TOUCH THE WORLD AS INTENDED, AND THAT WE WILL BE AMONGST THOSE WHO CARRY THE GOOD NEWS OF JESUS CHRIST TO OTHERS.

OUR PRAYER IS THAT MERCY, GRACE AND GOODNESS WILL FOLLOW US ALL THE DAYS OF OUR LIVES AND THAT OUR NEIGHBOURHOODS AND COMMUNITIES WILL KNOW THE SAVING GRACE AND FREEDOM THAT ONLY HEAVEN OFFERS.

MAY WE ALL COME TO KNOW THE ONE WHO WATCHES OVER US AND IN TURN, WATCH OVER ONE ANOTHER. OUR PRAYER IS THAT WE WILL ALLOW OURSELVES TO BE HIS PLANTING AND THAT TOGETHER, WE WILL ALL STAND ONE DAY AS A BEAUTIFUL, MATURE, RISEN SISTERHOOD OF DAUGHTERS WHO UNDERSTOOD THE DAYS WE WERE ENTRUSTED WITH."

c o n t e n t s

I AM
SIST
ERH
OOD

"I AM SISTERHOOD IS A DECLARATION. A DECLARATION THAT IS BOLD AND STRONG, QUIET AND CONFIDENT. A DECLARATION ABOUT VALUE AND IDENTITY, PURPOSE AND MISSION. IT IS A DECLARATION INTENTIONAL IN REACH AND EMBRACE. IT TRANSCENDS CULTURE AND CREED, AGE AND STATUS, PREJUDICE AND PREFERENCE.

IT'S A DECLARATION THAT POSITIONS ITSELF AMID AWARENESS AND RESPONSIBILITY, CONCERN AND CARE, INJUSTICE AND SOLUTION. A DECLARATION ULTIMATELY CONCERNED WITH THE WELFARE OF THE WORLD AND HER INHABITANTS. IT HAS COURAGEOUSLY WOVEN ITS WAY THROUGH TIME AND HISTORY AND CONTINUES TO WEAVE ITSELF ACROSS OUR LIVES AND FUTURE.

IT IS OUR COLLECTIVE HERE AND NOW - AND BELONGS TO ANY FEMININE SOUL, WHO SOMEHOW BELIEVES THAT SHE WAS BORN FOR MORE THAN WHAT IS TEMPORAL AND FLEETING. IT'S FOR WOMEN OF ALL AGES AND BACKGROUND, PERSONALITY AND STYLE, COLOUR AND VIBRANCY. IT'S FOR THE BOLD AND BODACIOUS, THE DEMURE AND UNASSUMING. IT'S THE SISTERHOOD THAT PERHAPS HEAVEN IMAGINED WHEN A VERY INTENTIONAL CREATOR CREATED HIS GIRLS. IT'S STRONG AND BEAUTIFUL, FEMININE AND GRACIOUS, AUTHORITATIVE AND GENTLE AND ABOVE ALL ELSE, WELCOMES THE BROKEN AND DISCARDED.

WHICHEVER WAY YOU SEE OR UNDERSTAND IT, IT IS A GROWING MOVEMENT OF WOMEN ACROSS THE EARTH. OUR HOPE IS THAT IN READING AND ABSORBING THE STORIES AND VISUALS IN THIS BOOK THAT YOUR HEART WILL BE ENLARGED AND BLESSED." © 2009

Bobbie Houston

SHE IS ONE, SHE IS MANY
AN INVITATION TO PRAYER

Empathy identifies with, and feels compassion towards the challenges and difficulties of another. This simple book and visual expression seeks to position our beloved global sisters before us. It lists the many nations and regions in which they are planted and captures a tiny glimpse of their beauty, potential and value. Many of these precious women face cultural, social and political challenge - and many are assailed by forces that need to incite concern and outrage.

Like us, they have hopes and dreams for their children and families. Like us, they have God-given gift and measure. Like us, they have been planted in time and history and deserve the opportunity to fulfil their own personal calling and destiny.

The Colour Sisterhood is in essence, a humanitarian movement. It is about everyday women using what is in their hand to make a difference. It is about raising awareness, standing in the gap and finding solution for those who have no voice, or for those who need a helping hand.

I believe that no genuine, heartfelt and earnest prayer goes unheard and my prayer and intent is that God's Spirit will prompt you to pray for various women and nations. There is space for you to pen your own dreams and desires, there is space for you to include your own family and friends that you are believing for, and there is space in and around the various regions for you to note whatever God places upon your heart.

SHE IS ONE, SHE IS MANY describes the sisterhood perfectly. A number of years ago I added to the Colour language: "If one woman can change her world, imagine what ONE COMPANY of women can do". That statement was back in the day when we were still imagining such a movement. Today, that movement and global sisterhood exists and TOGETHER there is no limit to what we can accomplish in Christ.

Jesus came to bring life and life in abundance. Let's be "our sister's keepers" and let's believe that prayer will displace darkness, open the heavens and cause His Love to prevail.

Bobbie Houston, 2012

Psalm 37:3-11 (NIV)

"TRUST IN THE LORD AND DO GOOD; DWELL IN THE LAND AND
ENJOY SAFE PASTURE. DELIGHT YOURSELF IN THE LORD AND HE
WILL GIVE YOU THE DESIRES OF YOUR HEART. COMMIT YOUR WAY
TO THE LORD; TRUST IN HIM AND HE WILL DO THIS: HE WILL MAKE
YOUR RIGHTEOUSNESS SHINE LIKE THE DAWN, THE JUSTICE OF
YOUR CAUSE LIKE THE NOONDAY SUN. BE STILL BEFORE THE LORD
AND WAIT PATIENTLY FOR HIM; DO NOT FRET WHEN MEN SUCCEED
IN THEIR WAYS, WHEN THEY CARRY OUT THEIR WICKED SCHEMES.
REFRAIN FROM ANGER AND TURN FROM WRATH; DO NOT FRET - IT
LEADS ONLY TO EVIL. FOR EVIL MEN WILL BE CUT OFF, BUT THOSE
WHO HOPE IN THE LORD WILL INHERIT THE LAND. A LITTLE WHILE,
AND THE WICKED WILL BE NO MORE; THOUGH YOU LOOK FOR THEM,
THEY WILL NOT BE FOUND. BUT THE MEEK WILL INHERIT THE LAND
AND ENJOY GREAT PEACE."

MY DREAMS/ & DESIRES

MY **CONVICTIONS**/ & BELIEFS

---

nations near & far

AUSTRALIA .
NEW ZEALAND .

warrior, princess, daughter.

My name is April. I fell pregnant with our first child. We were so excited, the doctor had confirmed it and it was true. My husband Nathan and I were ready for this new season together, but little did we know what really awaited us. We were smiling uncontrollably as we took our first ultrasound. We were able to see our little baby, hear her heartbeat, watch her move. We went snap crazy on our own camera, taking photos of the ultrasound photo in front of my tummy. It wasn't long after this that I got a phone call from our doctor. He said that the screening had shown there was a problem with our little baby. We were unclear on what was happening, but that day we began a heartbreaking journey. We soon discovered that our little baby girl, who we had named Sienna Hope had a serious heart problem. The doctors made sure we knew how serious the problem was and told us that the chances of a healthy baby, or even a baby at all, were very low. // The day it all hit home, was the day one of the nurses asked if we wanted to terminate our pregnancy. I couldn't believe this was happening to us, and yet without any thought or hesitation, both Nathan and I chose to walk this journey out and believe God for a miracle. // Week by week we took the scans and week by week the tests showed that Sienna was getting worse. At 32 weeks my placenta came away and I went straight to the hospital. By the time they realised what the problem was, I was in a critical state and was rushed into an emergency caesarean. As they wheeled me in, Nathan said one last time "Well, this is our chance for a miracle". We stood in faith. // When I woke up, my husband by my side, I learned that our beautiful little baby girl, Sienna Hope, had bypassed earth and gone straight to heaven. In all truth it was a heartbreaking moment in our lives, one that no one would wish upon another, but I have to say, it was a season and moment where I discovered God in a way I would perhaps not have known. Life isn't always perfect and there are things that we may never understand this side of eternity, but that day we began a journey of healing... and discovered a sense of devotion, faith and trust that we had never known. // Today, we have two beautiful children - a little boy and a little girl. We stand in awe of how great our God is, how supportive family and friends can be and we know with confidence that one day we will meet and see Sienna again.

sienna's story
SYDNEY/AUSTRALIA

ONE **LOVE**/
ONE **HEART**/
ONE **SISTER**
HOOD/

Our prayer is that women would know their value and worth. That they would continue to rise up and speak on behalf of those who have no voice. That there would be freedom from domestic violence and abuse. That there would be freedom from disease and poverty. That the government would have wisdom and strength. That the disadvantaged and disempowered women would find favour and freedom. That there would be harmony and peace between the different cultural groups. That the church would impact their community and be a voice for the voiceless in the nation and the world. That there would be continued economic stability. That all people would come to know the saving love of Jesus Christ.

PRAY FOR: PEACE. VALUE. DIGNITY. JUSTICE. SALVATION. **PRAY AGAINST:** HUMAN TRAFFICKING. POVERTY. DISCRIMINATION. DOMESTIC VIOLENCE. CORRUPTION. RACISM. ABUSE. DEPRESSION.

OUR **PRAYER**/
AUSTRALIA &
NEW ZEALAND

YOUR **PRAYER**/

melanesia

FIJI .
PAPUA NEW GUINEA .
SOLOMON ISLANDS .
VANUATU .

isaiah 51:5
(NIV)

"MY RIGHTEOUSNESS DRAWS NEAR SPEEDILY, MY SALVATION IS ON THE WAY, AND MY ARM WILL BRING JUSTICE TO THE NATIONS. THE ISLANDS WILL LOOK TO ME AND WAIT IN HOPE FOR MY ARM."

micronesia

- KIRIBATI
- MARSHALL ISLANDS
- MICRONESIA (FEDERATED STATES OF)
- NAURU
- PALAU

beautiful, beloved, believed in.

polynesia

SAMOA · TONGA · TUVALU ·

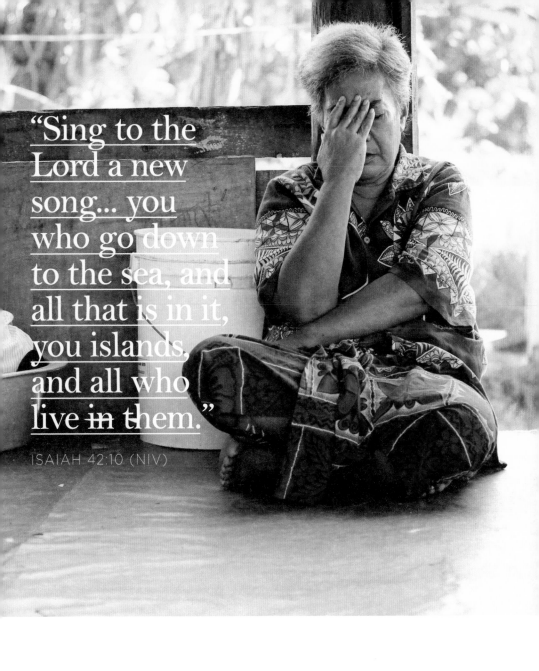

"Sing to the Lord a new song... you who go down to the sea, and all that is in it, you islands, and all who live in them."

ISAIAH 42:10 (NIV)

PRAY FOR: PEACE. VALUE. DIGNITY. JUSTICE. SALVATION. ECONOMIC STABILITY. POLITICAL STABILITY. **PRAY AGAINST:** POVERTY. ABUSE. DOMESTIC VIOLENCE. DISCRIMINATION. CORRUPTION. VIOLENCE. DISEASE.

OUR **PRAYER**/
MELANESIA, MICRONESIA
& POLYNESIA

YOUR **PRAYER**/

_____

_____

_____

_____

_____

_____

_____

_____

_____

southern africa

ANGOLA .
BOTSWANA .
LESOTHO .
MALAWI .
MOZAMBIQUE .
NAMIBIA .
SOUTH AFRICA .
SWAZILAND .
ZAMBIA .
ZIMBABWE .

"...THE WOMEN WERE COURAGEOUS, PERSISTENT, ENTHUSIASTIC, INDEFATIGABLE... 'WHEN THE WOMEN BEGIN TO TAKE AN ACTIVE PART IN THE STRUGGLE, NO POWER ON EARTH CAN STOP US FROM ACHIEVING FREEDOM IN OUR LIFETIME.'"

nelson mandela

'Long Walk to Freedom', Nelson Mandela,
reproduced by permission of Little, Brown Book Group.

trusted & empowered.

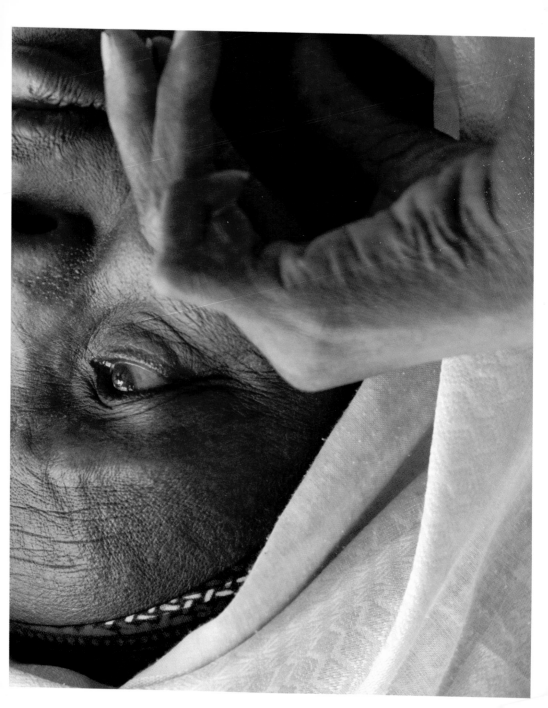

PRAY FOR: PEACE. VALUE. DIGNITY. JUSTICE. SALVATION. POLITICAL STABILITY. RECONCILIATION. **PRAY AGAINST:** POVERTY. FAMINE. DROUGHT. DISCRIMINATION. HUMAN TRAFFICKING. DOMESTIC VIOLENCE. HIV/AIDS. DISEASE.

OUR **PRAYER**/
SOUTHERN AFRICA

YOUR **PRAYER**/

_____

_____

_____

_____

_____

_____

_____

_____

_____

Zoleka's story

Challenges: Zoleka never knew her father. Her mother died when she was five, leaving her to be brought up by her grandmother. After falling pregnant, she had to leave her last year of school. The baby's father took Zoleka to join his parents in South Africa. Living in a township in Cape Town, she lived on what people gave her to hand-wash their clothes. Soon after arriving, her boyfriend brought another girlfriend home, who slept on the bed while Zoleka slept on the floor. A month after her baby boy was born, the father and his new girlfriend left. // Rescue: Alone and desperate, she started seeking God, and found Jesus at Hillsong Church, Cape Town soon after. // Thankful: for people who believe in her and a God who has given her life new hope and purpose.

"...to bestow on them a crown of beauty instead of ashes.

ISAIAH 61:3 (NIV

central africa

CAMEROON .
CENTRAL AFRICAN REPUBLIC .
CHAD .
CONGO .
DEMOCRATIC REPUBLIC,
OF THE CONGO .
EQUATORIAL GUINEA .
GABON .
SAO TOME AND PRINCIPE .

matthew 6:5-8
(NIV)

"And when you pray, do not be like the hypocrites, for they love to pray standing in the synagogues and on the street corners to be seen by others. Truly I tell you, they have received their reward in full. But when you pray, go into your room, close the door and pray to your Father, who is unseen. Then your Father, who sees what is done in secret, will reward you. And when you pray, do not keep on babbling like pagans, for they think they will be heard because of their many words. Do not be like them, for your Father knows what you need before you ask him."

mercy, truth & grace.

eastern africa

BURUNDI .
COMOROS .
DJIBOUTI .
ERITREA .
ETHIOPIA .
KENYA .
MADAGASCAR .
MAURITIUS .
RWANDA .
SEYCHELLES .
SOMALIA .
UGANDA .
UNITED REPUBLIC OF TANZANIA .

"A woman's beauty is not just in her face."

SOMALI PROVERB

everline's story

Injustice: Abducted by rebels at age 15 on her way to school. // Suffering: Coerced into becoming a child soldier – kill or be killed. Beaten unconscious and left for dead. Given to rebel leaders as a sex slave. Infected with HIV virus. Became a child mother. Abandoned by family and community. // Rescue: Watoto – Living Hope, 2008. // Miracle: Receiving and giving forgiveness. Realising her children were not an accident but a gift from God. // Today: Everline is a tailor, buys her own food, pays her own rent and sends her children to school. Her dream is for her children to have a better life than she had. // Gratitude: Her heart overflows with thanksgiving for the sisters she'll never meet that came alongside her, so that she could be restored to dignity.

justice & freedom.

PRAY FOR: PEACE. VALUE. DIGNITY. JUSTICE. SALVATION. POLITICAL STABILITY. RECONCILIATION. **PRAY AGAINST:** CIVIL WAR AND RAPE. POVERTY. FAMINE. DROUGHT. DISCRIMINATION. HUMAN TRAFFICKING. DOMESTIC VIOLENCE. MUTILATION. PERSECUTION OF CHRISTIANS AND THE CHURCH. HIV/AIDS. CORRUPTION. DISEASE.

OUR **PRAYER**/
CENTRAL &
EASTERN AFRICA

YOUR **PRAYER**/

_____

_____

_____

_____

_____

_____

_____

_____

western africa

BENIN .
BURKINA FASO .
CAPE VERDE .
CÔTE D'IVOIRE .
GAMBIA .
GHANA .
GUINEA .
GUINEA BISSAU .
LIBERIA .
MALI .
MAURITANIA .
NIGER .
NIGERIA .
SENEGAL .
SIERRA LEONE .
TOGO .

"Blessed are the peacemakers, for they will be called children of God."

MATTHEW 5:9 (NIV)

leymah's story

"In the past we were silent, but after being killed, raped, dehumanized, and infected with diseases, and watching our children and families destroyed, war has taught us that the future lies in saying NO to violence and YES to peace! We will not relent until peace prevails." // Leymah Gbowee won the Nobel Peace Prize in 2011 after starting a peace movement amongst the women of her nation of Liberia, tragically torn apart by civil war. She brought the Christian and Muslim women together to pray for PEACE and to peacefully protest until the fighting parties had to make an agreement.

dignity & value.

PRAY FOR: PEACE. VALUE. DIGNITY. JUSTICE. SALVATION. POLITICAL STABILITY.
PRAY AGAINST: CIVIL WAR . POVERTY. FAMINE. DROUGHT. DISCRIMINATION. HUMAN
TRAFFICKING. DOMESTIC VIOLENCE. MUTILATION. PERSECUTION OF CHRISTIANS
AND THE CHURCH. HIV/AIDS. DISEASE.

OUR **PRAYER**/
WESTERN AFRICA

YOUR **PRAYER**/

northern africa

ALGERIA .
EGYPT .
LIBYA .
MOROCCO .
SOUTH SUDAN .
SUDAN .
TUNISIA .

"...SOMETHING NEW HAD TOUCHED THE WOMEN OF AFRICA, AND THEY BEGAN TO VOICE THEIR PRESENCE. WOMEN WERE STANDING UP, ABANDONING THE CROUCHED POSITIONS FROM WHICH THEIR LIFE-BREATH STIMULATED THE WOOD FIRES THAT BURNED UNDER THE EARTHENWARE POTS OF VEGETABLES THEY HAD GROWN AND HARVESTED. THE POTS, TOO, WERE THEIR HANDIWORK. STANDING UP STRAIGHT, WOMEN OF AFRICA STRETCHED THEIR HANDS TO THE GLOBAL SISTERHOOD OF LIFE-LOVING WOMEN. IN NO UNCERTAIN TERMS, AFRICAN WOMEN ANNOUNCED THEIR POSITION ON THE LIBERATION STRUGGLE AND THEIR SOLIDARITY WITH OTHER WOMEN."

mercy amba oduyoye

'Daughters of Anowa: African Women and Patriarchy', Orbis Books 1995

PRAY FOR: PEACE. VALUE. DIGNITY. JUSTICE. SALVATION. POLITICAL STABILITY.
PRAY AGAINST: CIVIL WAR. HONOUR KILLINGS. POVERTY. FAMINE. DISCRIMINATION. HUMAN TRAFFICKING. DOMESTIC VIOLENCE. MUTILATION. PERSECUTION OF CHRISTIANS AND THE CHURCH.

OUR **PRAYER**/
NORTHERN AFRICA

YOUR **PRAYER**/

northern europe

DENMARK .
FINLAND .
ICELAND .
NORWAY .
SWEDEN .

courage & worth.

Amos 5:14-15
(The Message)

"SEEK GOOD AND NOT EVIL—AND LIVE! YOU TALK ABOUT GOD, THE GOD-OF-THE-ANGEL-ARMIES, BEING YOUR BEST FRIEND. WELL, LIVE LIKE IT, AND MAYBE IT WILL HAPPEN. HATE EVIL AND LOVE GOOD, THEN WORK IT OUT IN THE PUBLIC SQUARE..."

western europe

AUSTRIA .
BELGIUM .
FRANCE .
GERMANY .
IRELAND .
LIECHTENSTEIN .
LUXEMBOURG .
MONACO .
NETHERLANDS .
SWITZERLAND .
UNITED KINGDOM OF GREAT BRITAIN
AND NORTHERN IRELAND .

Challenges: Barbara's husband died of cancer at 42 leaving her to raise four children and run the family farm on her own. She herself was diagnosed with breast cancer just a couple of years later and fought the disease for a number of years while continuing to run the farm and support her children. Through this all she never lost her sense of humour, strength to fight or spirit of adventure. // Faithfulness: She volunteered and supported her local church for 50 years in a small village in England. Rediscovering her faith later in life, she was heard to say that she wanted to die while everyone was in church worshiping God. She died on a Sunday morning in 1999 while her family was in church. // Legacy: Just an everyday woman, but one who has left a legacy of children, grandchildren and now great grandchildren who have been inspired to live life better because of her.

barbara's story
BORN 1920/UK

love & faithfulness.

PRAY FOR: PEACE. VALUE. DIGNITY. JUSTICE. SALVATION. POLITICAL STABILITY. ECONOMIC STABILITY. **PRAY AGAINST:** HUMAN TRAFFICKING. UNEMPLOYMENT. DISCRIMINATION. DOMESTIC VIOLENCE. CORRUPTION. RACISM. ABUSE. DISEASE. DEPRESSION.

OUR **PRAYER**/
NORTHERN EUROPE &
WESTERN EUROPE

YOUR **PRAYER**/

_____

_____

_____

_____

_____

_____

_____

_____

_____

eastern europe

BULGARIA .
CZECH REPUBLIC .
ESTONIA .
HUNGARY .
LATVIA .
LITHUANIA .
POLAND .
REPUBLIC OF MOLDOVA .
ROMANIA .
RUSSIAN FEDERATION .
SLOVAKIA .
UKRAINE .

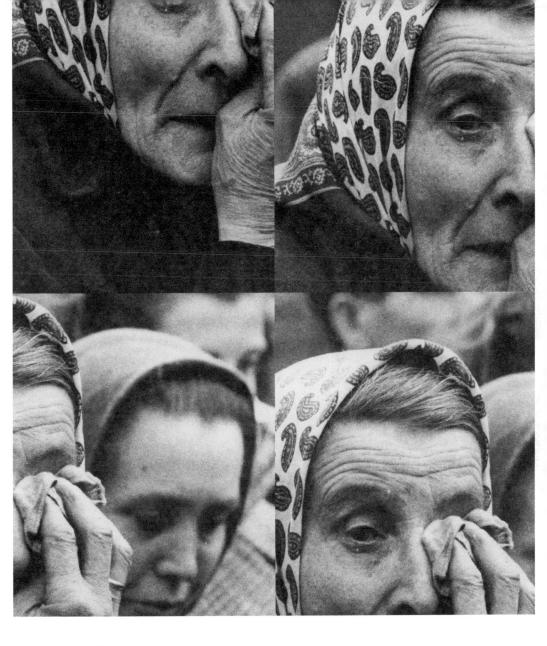

beauty for ashes.

PRAY FOR: PEACE. VALUE. DIGNITY. JUSTICE. SALVATION. POLITICAL STABILITY. ECONOMIC STABILITY. **PRAY AGAINST:** POVERTY. DISCRIMINATION. HUMAN TRAFFICKING. DOMESTIC VIOLENCE. CORRUPTION. CIVIL WAR. DEPRESSION. DRUG & ALCOHOL ABUSE.

OUR **PRAYER**/
EASTERN EUROPE

YOUR **PRAYER**/

_____

_____

_____

_____

_____

_____

_____

_____

_____

Age: 21 years // Birthplace: Ukraine. // Injustice: Offered a false job as a waitress in Greece, Libby was tricked, stripped of her documentation, raped and sold into the sex industry. Libby faced 8 months of being locked in a room and was forced to have sex with multiple men every day. She also suffered heavy beatings from customers and traffickers. // Rescue: November 2011, A21 Shelter Greece. // Miracle: Libby has learned to trust again, received Jesus Christ as her Saviour and has learned the power of forgiveness. Libby has now returned to her home country, holds a steady job as a gym instructor and is regularly involved in church.

libby's story

UKRAINE

*her name has been changed to protect her identity

"...to proclaim freedom for the captives..."

ISAIAH 61:1 (NIV)

mediterranean europe

ALBANIA .
ANDORRA .
BOSNIA AND HERZEGOVINA .
CROATIA .
CYPRUS .
GREECE .
ITALY .
MALTA .
MONTENEGRO .
PORTUGAL .
SAN MARINO .
SERBIA .
SLOVENIA .
SPAIN .
THE FORMER YUGOSLAV
REPUBLIC OF MACEDONIA .

Age: 43 // Challenges: Kalli's father, Greek by birth, was a well-known pimp and nightclub owner who trafficked narcotics and women in Cape Town. She was both physically and emotionally abused as a child and a teenager. Rejection, insecurity, and worthlessness was the only thing she knew. // Miracle: Miraculously her father was transformed by God and her family returned to Greece and began serving the Lord. // Opportunity: Kalli never forgot the pain and suffering of the victims of trafficking, but as a wife and mother of two children, she felt she had nothing to offer. She learned that the A21 Campaign had a shelter near her hometown of Thessaloniki, Greece. Fighting feelings of insecurity and questioning her abilities, she soon found herself by the side of victims of sex slavery, fighting for their protection and rights. The woman who said, "What can I do? I'm only a mum," soon found herself being a mother to those who had none. // Legacy: Today Kalli is a shelter coordinator for the A21 Thessaloniki shelter, redeeming her story and the legacy of her family by serving those victimised by the crime of human trafficking.

kalli's story
THESSALONIKI/GREECE

"HE HAS SHOWED YOU, O MAN, WHAT IS GOOD. AND WHAT DOES THE LORD REQUIRE OF YOU BUT TO DO JUSTLY, AND TO LOVE KINDNESS AND MERCY, AND TO HUMBLE YOURSELF AND WALK HUMBLY WITH YOUR GOD?"

micah 6:8
(AMP)

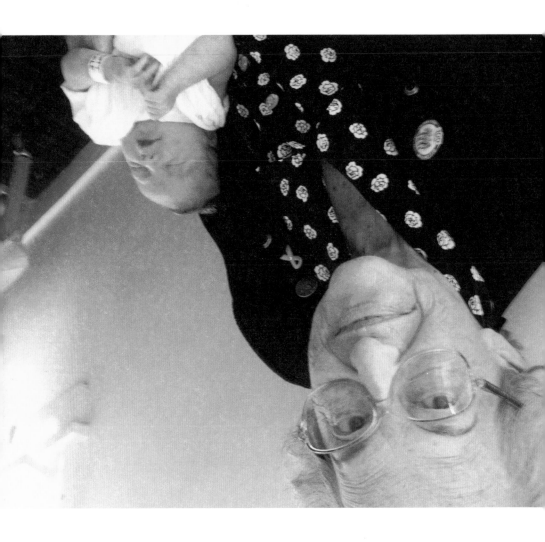

PRAY FOR: PEACE. VALUE. DIGNITY. JUSTICE. SALVATION. POLITICAL STABILITY. ECONOMIC STABILITY. **PRAY AGAINST:** HUMAN TRAFFICKING. UNEMPLOYMENT. DISCRIMINATION. DOMESTIC VIOLENCE. CORRUPTION. RACISM. DEPRESSION. ABUSE.

OUR **PRAYER**/
MEDITERRANEAN EUROPE

YOUR **PRAYER**/

"THIS IS THE KIND OF FAST DAY I'M AFTER: TO BREAK THE CHAINS OF INJUSTICE, GET RID OF EXPLOITATION IN THE WORKPLACE, FREE THE OPPRESSED, CANCEL DEBTS. WHAT I'M INTERESTED IN SEEING YOU DO IS: SHARING YOUR FOOD WITH THE HUNGRY, INVITING THE HOMELESS POOR INTO YOUR HOMES, PUTTING CLOTHES ON THE SHIVERING ILL-CLAD, BEING AVAILABLE TO YOUR OWN FAMILIES. DO THIS AND THE LIGHTS WILL TURN ON, AND YOUR LIVES WILL TURN AROUND AT ONCE.

Isaiah 58:6-14
(The Message)

YOUR RIGHTEOUSNESS WILL PAVE YOUR WAY. THE GOD OF GLORY WILL SECURE YOUR PASSAGE. THEN WHEN YOU PRAY, GOD WILL ANSWER. YOU'LL CALL OUT FOR HELP AND I'LL SAY, 'HERE I AM.' **A FULL LIFE IN THE EMPTIEST OF PLACES** "IF YOU GET RID OF UNFAIR PRACTICES, QUIT BLAMING VICTIMS, QUIT GOSSIPING ABOUT OTHER PEOPLE'S SINS, IF YOU ARE GENEROUS WITH THE HUNGRY AND START GIVING YOURSELVES TO THE DOWN-AND-OUT, YOUR LIVES WILL BEGIN TO

GLOW IN THE DARKNESS, YOUR
SHADOWED LIVES WILL BE
BATHED IN SUNLIGHT. I WILL
ALWAYS SHOW YOU WHERE TO
GO. I'LL GIVE YOU A FULL LIFE
IN THE EMPTIEST OF PLACES —
FIRM MUSCLES, STRONG
BONES. YOU'LL BE LIKE A WELL-
WATERED GARDEN, A GURGLING
SPRING THAT NEVER RUNS DRY.
YOU'LL USE THE OLD RUBBLE
OF PAST LIVES TO BUILD ANEW,
REBUILD THE FOUNDATIONS
FROM OUT OF YOUR PAST.
YOU'LL BE KNOWN AS THOSE
WHO CAN FIX ANYTHING,
RESTORE OLD RUINS, REBUILD
AND RENOVATE, MAKE THE
COMMUNITY LIVABLE AGAIN.

"IF YOU WATCH YOUR STEP ON THE SABBATH AND DON'T USE MY HOLY DAY FOR PERSONAL ADVANTAGE, IF YOU TREAT THE SABBATH AS A DAY OF JOY, GOD'S HOLY DAY AS A CELEBRATION, IF YOU HONOR IT BY REFUSING 'BUSINESS AS USUAL,' MAKING MONEY, RUNNING HERE AND THERE — THEN YOU'LL BE FREE TO ENJOY GOD! OH, I'LL MAKE YOU RIDE HIGH AND SOAR ABOVE IT ALL. I'LL MAKE YOU FEAST ON THE INHERITANCE OF YOUR ANCESTOR JACOB." YES! GOD SAYS SO!

north america

CANADA .
MEXICO .
UNITED STATES OF AMERICA .

"If we are to better the future we must disturb the present."

CATHERINE BOOTH

meredith's story

When I moved to New York, I was trying to get away from the party lifestyle in L.A. I was the typical party girl, the person that everyone invited because they knew I was going to be crazy. I did a lot of drugs. I think I felt like I could be young forever. I was hoping to find a new life in New York. I was hoping to find something more real. I got here but I was still going out to nightclubs and doing drugs. I started to spend a lot of time by myself, just locked up in my apartment sleeping in late, missing work. Instead of feeling more grounded in New York, I was just feeling more alone. I reached out to a friend of mine and said "I haven't spoken to you in seven years. I heard you go to church. I want to go with you, are you going this Sunday?" And she wrote back "yes, I go to church and of course you can come with me." As soon as I walked in I was just blown away. I was trying to focus on what they were talking about and singing and I just felt my heart start to break. I felt God calling me back, as clear as day. I heard a voice saying "Now's the time, I've been waiting for you." It was the warmest most comforting voice, and I just said yes, I'm going to change my life right now. I have made so many mistakes but I finally feel like I've been set free. I don't have to keep moving from here to there to find the answer, I can just be here. I feel at home now!

freedom for the captive.

PRAY FOR: PEACE. VALUE. DIGNITY. JUSTICE. SALVATION. ECONOMIC STABILITY.
PRAY AGAINST: HUMAN TRAFFICKING. POVERTY. DISCRIMINATION. DOMESTIC
VIOLENCE. CORRUPTION. RACISM. VIOLENCE. ABUSE. DISEASE. DEPRESSION.

YOUR **PRAYER/**

central america

BELIZE .
COSTA RICA .
EL SALVADOR .
GUATEMALA .
HONDURAS .
NICARAGUA .
PANAMA .

"IN THE SAME WAY, THE SPIRIT HELPS US IN OUR WEAKNESS. WE DO NOT KNOW WHAT WE OUGHT TO PRAY FOR, BUT THE SPIRIT HIMSELF INTERCEDES FOR US THROUGH WORDLESS GROANS. AND HE WHO SEARCHES OUR HEARTS KNOWS THE MIND OF THE SPIRIT, BECAUSE THE SPIRIT INTERCEDES FOR GOD'S PEOPLE IN ACCORDANCE WITH THE WILL OF GOD."

romans 8: 26-27
(NIV)

the caribbean
ANTIGUA AND BARBUDA .
BAHAMAS .
BARBADOS .
BERMUDA .
CUBA .
DOMINICA .
DOMINICAN REPUBLIC .
GRENADA .
HAITI .
JAMAICA .
SAINT KITTS AND NEVIS .
SAINT LUCIA .
SAINT VINCENT AND THE GRENADINES .
TRINIDAD AND TOBAGO .

PRAY FOR: PEACE. VALUE. DIGNITY. JUSTICE. SALVATION. ECONOMIC STABILITY. POLITICAL STABILITY. **PRAY AGAINST:** POVERTY. DISCRIMINATION. DOMESTIC VIOLENCE. HUMAN TRAFFICKING. CORRUPTION. VIOLENCE. DRUG TRAFFICKING. DISEASE. ABUSE.

OUR **PRAYER**/
CENTRAL AMERICA &
CARIBBEAN

YOUR **PRAYER**/

---

south america

ARGENTINA .
BOLIVIA (PLURINATIONAL STATE OF) .
BRAZIL .
CHILE .
COLOMBIA .
ECUADOR .
GUYANA .
PARAGUAY .
PERU .
SURINAME .
URUGUAY .
VENEZUELA (BOLIVARIAN
REPUBLIC OF) .

blessed are the peacemakers.

Isaiah 61:1-4
(NIV)

"THE SPIRIT OF THE SOVEREIGN LORD IS ON ME, BECAUSE THE LORD HAS ANOINTED ME TO PROCLAIM GOOD NEWS TO THE POOR. HE HAS SENT ME TO BIND UP THE BROKENHEARTED, TO PROCLAIM FREEDOM FOR THE CAPTIVES AND RELEASE FROM DARKNESS FOR THE PRISONERS, TO PROCLAIM THE YEAR OF THE LORD'S FAVOR AND THE DAY OF VENGEANCE OF OUR GOD, TO COMFORT ALL WHO MOURN, AND PROVIDE FOR THOSE WHO GRIEVE IN ZION — TO BESTOW ON THEM A CROWN OF BEAUTY INSTEAD OF ASHES, THE OIL OF JOY INSTEAD OF MOURNING, AND A GARMENT OF PRAISE INSTEAD OF A SPIRIT OF DESPAIR. THEY WILL BE CALLED OAKS OF RIGHTEOUSNESS, A PLANTING OF THE LORD FOR THE DISPLAY OF HIS SPLENDOR. THEY WILL REBUILD THE ANCIENT RUINS AND RESTORE THE PLACES LONG DEVASTATED; THEY WILL RENEW THE RUINED CITIES THAT HAVE BEEN DEVASTATED FOR GENERATIONS."

Luke 4: 18, 20-21
(NIV) paraphrased

"THE SPIRIT OF THE LORD IS ON ME, BECAUSE HE HAS ANOINTED ME..." THEN HE ROLLED UP THE SCROLL, GAVE IT BACK TO THE ATTENDANT AND SAT DOWN..." HE BEGAN BY SAYING TO THEM, 'TODAY THIS SCRIPTURE IS FULFILLED IN YOUR HEARING.'"

a mother's story

The "Madres de Plazo de Mayo" were a company of women whose children had "disappeared" during the dictatorship of the 1970's. They brought their grief and their desire for justice into the public arena, protesting in the main squares by wearing photos of their children around their necks. They were instrumental in bringing the military to justice in many circumstances through a peaceful protest. Many of them never found out what happened to their children.

"...strength and dignity are her clothing..."
PROVERBS 31:25 (AMP)

PRAY FOR: PEACE. VALUE. DIGNITY. JUSTICE. SALVATION. ECONOMIC STABILITY. POLITICAL STABILITY. **PRAY AGAINST:** POVERTY. CORRUPTION. DISCRIMINATION. DOMESTIC VIOLENCE. HUMAN TRAFFICKING. VIOLENCE. DRUG TRAFFICKING. DISEASE. ABUSE

OUR **PRAYER**/
SOUTH AMERICA

YOUR **PRAYER**/

middle east

IRAN (ISLAMIC REPUBLIC OF) .
IRAQ .
ISRAEL .
JORDAN .
KUWAIT .
LEBANON .
OMAN .
PALESTINE .
QATAR .
SAUDI ARABIA .
SYRIAN ARAB REPUBLIC .
TURKEY .
UNITED ARAB EMIRATES .
YEMEN .

"AND I WILL SOW HER FOR MYSELF ANEW IN THE LAND, AND I WILL HAVE LOVE, PITY, AND MERCY FOR HER WHO HAD NOT OBTAINED LOVE, PITY, AND MERCY; AND I WILL SAY TO THOSE WHO WERE NOT MY PEOPLE, YOU ARE MY PEOPLE, AND THEY SHALL SAY, YOU ARE MY GOD!"

hosea 2:23
(AMP)

PRAY FOR: PEACE. VALUE. DIGNITY. JUSTICE. SALVATION. POLITICAL STABILITY. ECONOMIC STABILITY. **PRAY AGAINST:** WAR AND TERROR. DISCRIMINATION. POVERTY. HUMAN TRAFFICKING. DOMESTIC VIOLENCE. PERSECUTION OF CHRISTIANS AND THE CHURCH. VIOLENCE. HONOUR KILLINGS.

OUR **PRAYER/**
MIDDLE EAST

YOUR **PRAYER/**

_____

_____

_____

_____

_____

_____

_____

_____

_____

southern asia

AFGHANISTAN .
BANGLADESH .
BHUTAN .
INDIA .
MALDIVES .
NEPAL .
PAKISTAN .
SRI LANKA .

"What can
you do to
promote
world peace?
Go home
and love
your family."

MOTHER THERESA

PRAY FOR: VALUE. PEACE. DIGNITY. JUSTICE. SALVATION. **PRAY AGAINST:** POVERTY. DISCRIMINATION. MISSING GIRLS/WOMEN DUE TO SEX SELECTION AND INFANTICIDE. HUMAN TRAFFICKING. VIOLENCE AND ABUSE. PERSECUTION OF CHRISTIANS. DISEASE. HONOUR KILLINGS. WAR AND TERROR.

OUR **PRAYER**/
SOUTHERN ASIA

YOUR **PRAYER**/

_____

_____

_____

_____

_____

_____

_____

_____

_____

pooja's story

Name: Pooja // Age: 12 // Location: Mumbai Streets // Challenge: Her parents earn a living by making bamboo baskets. With no proper shelter her family live on the streets and barely make ends meet. She was ridiculed at school by the other children for not being clean and her family couldn't afford to buy her the books she needed. As a result Pooja eventually dropped out. // Rescue: She started attending a VISION RESCUE school bus once a day and after two years attendance and much persuasion her family decided to send her back to school. Pooja is now an excited student who has big dreams for the future.

one love...

western asia

ARMENIA .
AZERBAIJAN .
BAHRAIN .
BELARUS .
GEORGIA .

central asia

KAZAKHSTAN .
KYRGYZSTAN .
TAJIKISTAN .
TURKMENISTAN .
UZBEKISTAN .

"THE LORD GIVES THE WORD [OF POWER]; THE WOMEN WHO BEAR AND PUBLISH [THE NEWS] ARE A GREAT HOST."

psalm 68:11
(AMP)

PRAY FOR: VALUE. PEACE. DIGNITY. JUSTICE. SALVATION. POLITICAL STABILITY. ECONOMIC STABILITY. **PRAY AGAINST:** WAR. POVERTY. DISCRIMINATION. HUMAN TRAFFICKING. DOMESTIC VIOLENCE. PERSECUTION OF CHRISTIANS AND THE CHURCH. CORRUPTION. ABUSE. CIVIL WAR.

OUR **PRAYER/**
WESTERN &
CENTRAL ASIA

YOUR **PRAYER/**

_____

_____

_____

_____

_____

_____

_____

_____

_____

northern asia

CHINA .
DEMOCRATIC PEOPLE'S REPUBLIC
OF KOREA .
HONG KONG .
JAPAN .
MONGOLIA .
REPUBLIC OF KOREA .

"Women hold up half the sky."

PRAY FOR: VALUE. PEACE. DIGNITY. JUSTICE. SALVATION. **PRAY AGAINST:** POVERTY. DISCRIMINATION. MISSING GIRLS/WOMEN DUE TO SEX SELECTION AND INFANTICIDE. HUMAN TRAFFICKING. VIOLENCE AND ABUSE. PERSECUTION OF CHRISTIANS AND THE CHURCH. CORRUPTION. WAR AND TERROR.

OUR **PRAYER/**
NORTHERN ASIA

YOUR **PRAYER/**

south east asia

BRUNEI DARUSSALAM .
CAMBODIA .
INDONESIA .
LAO PEOPLE'S DEMOCRATIC REPUBLIC .
MALAYSIA .
MYANMAR .
PHILIPPINES .
SINGAPORE .
THAILAND .
TIMOR-LESTE .
VIET NAM .

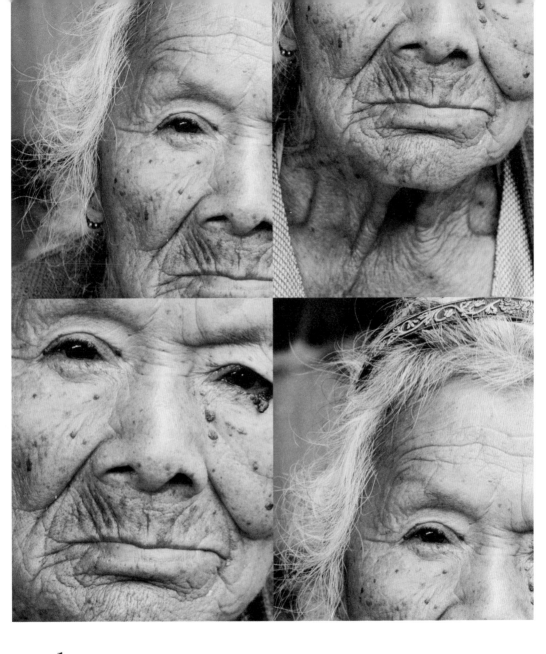

one heart...

Somaly, born into poverty in Cambodia, sold into slavery at the age of 6, raped and beaten for years until escaping. She now fights on behalf of those who are still enslaved. She fights because "I don't want to go without leaving a trace."

somaly's story
CAMBODIA/ASIA

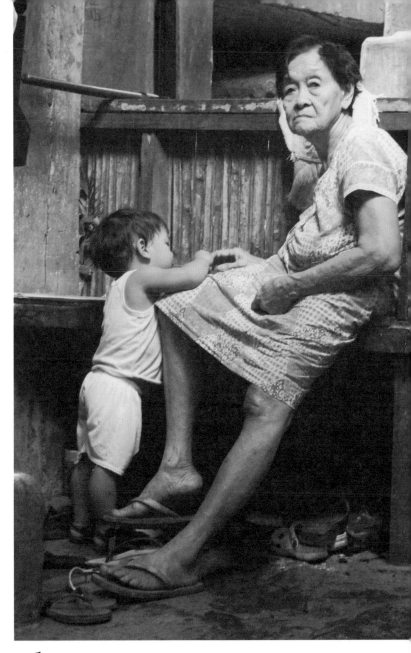

one sisterhood.

"THE EDUCATION & EMPOWERMENT OF WOMEN THROUGHOUT THE WORLD CAN NOT FAIL TO RESULT IN A MORE CARING, TOLERANT, JUST AND PEACEFUL LIFE FOR ALL."

Aung San Suu Kyi

(1991 Nobel Peace Prize for non-violent struggle for democracy and human rights)

hebrews 12: 1-3

(The Message)

"DO YOU SEE WHAT THIS MEANS—ALL THESE PIONEERS WHO BLAZED THE WAY, ALL THESE VETERANS CHEERING US ON? IT MEANS WE'D BETTER GET ON WITH IT. STRIP DOWN, START RUNNING—AND NEVER QUIT! NO EXTRA SPIRITUAL FAT, NO PARASITIC SINS. KEEP YOUR EYES ON JESUS, WHO BOTH BEGAN AND FINISHED THIS RACE WE'RE IN. STUDY HOW HE DID IT. BECAUSE HE NEVER LOST SIGHT OF WHERE HE WAS HEADED—THAT EXHILARATING FINISH IN AND WITH GOD—HE COULD PUT UP WITH ANYTHING ALONG THE WAY: CROSS, SHAME, WHATEVER. AND NOW HE'S THERE, IN THE PLACE OF HONOR, RIGHT ALONGSIDE GOD. WHEN YOU FIND YOURSELVES FLAGGING IN YOUR FAITH, GO OVER THAT STORY AGAIN, ITEM BY ITEM, THAT LONG LITANY OF HOSTILITY HE PLOWED THROUGH. THAT WILL SHOOT ADRENALINE INTO YOUR SOULS!"

PRAY FOR: VALUE. PEACE. DIGNITY. JUSTICE. SALVATION. POLITICAL STABILITY. ECONOMIC STABILITY. **PRAY AGAINST:** POVERTY. DISCRIMINATION. CORRUPTION. HUMAN TRAFFICKING. VIOLENCE AND ABUSE. PERSECUTION OF CHRISTIANS AND THE CHURCH.

YOUR **PRAYER**/

ISRAEL
GREECE
TURKEY
ITALY
ARMENIA AZERBAIJAN
ROMANIA
GEORGIA
MOLDOVA
UKRAINE
BELARUS NETHERLANDS
KAZAKHSTAN GERMANY

the prayer map

THE PRAYER MAP IS AN INITIATIVE OF THE COLOUR SISTERHOOD AND COLOUR CONFERENCE AND CAN BE SOURCED ONLINE AT www.coloursisterhood.com

ITS MAJOR CONCERN IS THE ESCALATING GLOBAL CRIME OF HUMAN TRAFFICKING AND ALLOWS FOR THE DOWNLOAD OF INDIVIDUAL NATIONS THAT ARE SOURCE COUNTRIES, DESTINATIONS, PORTS AND BORDERS WHERE TRAFFICKING OCCURS. EACH PRAYER MAP GIVES A BRIEF BACKGROUND TO THE SOCIAL CHALLENGES FACING EACH NATION AND OUTLINES PRAYER POINTS.

THE GOAL IS AWARENESS, PREVENTION, RESCUE AND RESTORATION. THE GOAL IS TO SABOTAGE, THROUGH EFFECTIVE PRAYER, THE PLANS OF THE TRAFFICKERS AND THE EVIL FORCES BEHIND THIS GRAVE INJUSTICE AGAINST HUMANITY. THE GOAL IS FOR LIGHT TO PREVAIL, DARKNESS TO TREMBLE AND THE LOVE OF GOD TO RESCUE AND RESTORE THE PRECIOUS LIVES OF MEN, WOMEN AND CHILDREN WHO HAVE FALLEN VICTIM.

GO ONLINE AND CHOOSE WHICHEVER NATION(S) ARE OF CONCERN TO YOU. ON BEHALF OF THOSE RESCUED THUS FAR, THANK YOU!

THE HEARTS/
BEHIND THIS BOOK
THE HOUSE . THE COLOUR SISTERHOOD . THE COLOUR CONFERENCE

the house

Hillsong is a local church in Australia with global campuses in major cities around the world. It is a Christ-centered church, with a genuine heart to bring the inclusive love, redemptive message and social concern of Christ to the communities, cities and nations of the world. People from all walks of life and society are the everyday face of Hillsong. The church was founded in 1983 by Brian and Bobbie Houston and is part of the Australian Christian Churches. For more info visit **www.hillsong.com**

the colour sisterhood

The Colour Sisterhood represents many thousands of everyday women around the world, who have aligned their heart and spirit to "be the change" in the worlds they inhabit. Our focus is both local and global. Women are encouraged to respond to the needs in their local communities - and then our strengths combine to collectively address and bring solution to various major global challenges and injustice. For more info visit **www.coloursisterhood.com**

the colour conference

The "Colour Your World Women's Conference" commenced in 1997 and is hosted by Bobbie Houston and Hillsong Church. It is in essence an outflow of Hillsong's local Sisterhood ministry. It gathers leaders and women from every age and walk of life and its core value is to "place value upon womanhood" and champion the potential within women. Bobbie and the Hillsong team currently host this conference in Sydney, London, Kiev and Cape Town. For more info visit **www.colourconference.com**

REFLECTIONS/
& SELAH MOMENTS

"IN THIS MANNER, THEREFORE, PRAY: OUR FATHER IN HEAVEN, HALLOWED BE YOUR NAME. YOUR KINGDOM COME. YOUR WILL BE DONE ON EARTH AS *IT IS* IN HEAVEN. GIVE US THIS DAY OUR DAILY BREAD. AND FORGIVE US OUR DEBTS, AS WE FORGIVE OUR DEBTORS. AND DO NOT LEAD US INTO TEMPTATION, BUT DELIVER US FROM THE EVIL ONE. FOR YOURS IS THE KINGDOM AND THE POWER AND THE GLORY FOREVER. AMEN."

matthew 6:9-13
(NKJV)

t h a n k   y o u

I wish to thank those who volunteered their gift and passion to make this book a reality. Special appreciation in particular to Catherine and Noodle for their tireless devotion to all it represents. Thank you to those who graciously donated time, effort, research hours and photos to this project. May eternity bear witness to lives rescued and transformed because this prayer journal/tool prompted concern for sisters near and far. God bless you. Bobbie

a c k n o w l e d g e m e n t s

Thank you to all of the people that donated their photos so that we could depict the beautiful diversity of the world's women: Natalie Chapple/ Carlos Darby/ Robert Fergusson/ Mystique Sea Flores/ Danika Haeusler/ Chihiro Hagiwara/ Joel Houston/ I-HEART/ Matt Johnson/ Anders Kjondal/ Salomon Ligthelm/ Bel Litchfield (Trigger Happy Images)/ Tessa Moerchen/ Rahkela Nardella/ Sasha Nesterenko/ Josh O'Rourke/ Bel Pangburn/ Ed Peers/ Caroline Presbury/ Leonie Quayle/ Niyah Rahmaan/ Dayana Rocha/ Anthony Sider/ Glenn Stewart/ Catherine Thambiratnam/ David Thambiratnam/ Kishan Thambiratnam/ Laura Toginavalu/ Vera Toginavalu/ Vlad Vasylkevych.

Thank you to all of the people that donated their time to research for this project: Hannah Aarget/ Carl-Hugo Ander/ Ruth Athanasio/ Johanna Barker/ Renae Bartley/ Ros Campbell/ Karalee Fielding/ Karen Greybe/ Julie Haworth/ Carmen Helm/ Jemima Honor/ Emily Hutchins/ Ashley Jones/ Shannon Kelly/ Daniel Lai/ Eleanor Lee/ Grace Mononela/ Josh Olsen/ Tash Parkes/ Jessica Pollock/ Simone Ridley/ Ricki Row/ Jessamine Sam/ Georgi Sheaf/ Juliette Spurling/ Esther Volstad/ Nikki Webb.

Thank you to all of the women whose stories have inspired us: April (and Sienna)/ Meredith/ Kalli/ Zoleka/ Pooja/ Barbara / Somaly / Leymah/ Everline/ Sasha.

index

ISBN 978-0-646-56965-9

First released at Colour Conference 2012
© 2011 Hillsong Church Ltd.

Published by Hillsong Music Australia.

Scripture quotations marked (NIV) are taken from the Holy Bible, New International Version®, NIV®.
Copyright © 1973, 1978, 1984, 2011 by Biblica, Inc.™ Used by permission of Zondervan.
All rights reserved worldwide. www.zondervan.com.

The "NIV" and "New International Version" are trademarks registered in the United States Patent and
Trademark Office by Biblica, Inc.™

Scripture quotations marked "NKJV™" are taken from the New King James Version®.
Copyright © 1982 by Thomas Nelson, Inc. Used by permission. All rights reserved.

Scripture quotations marked (AMP) are taken from the Amplified Bible, Copyright © 1954, 1958, 1962, 1964, 1965, 1987
by The Lockman Foundation. Used by permission.

Scripture quotations from THE MESSAGE. Copyright © by Eugene H. Peterson 1993, 1994, 1995, 1996, 2000, 2001, 2002.
Used by permission of NavPress Publishing Group.

Some photos provided by Getty Images

Cover & design by Nicole Scott (a.k.a. Noodle)

www.hillsong.com www.colourconference.com www.coloursisterhood.com
twitter: @hillsong @colourconf @coloursistahood
facebook.com/hillsong